Self-Regula
Workbook

Fun Activities, CBT Exercises, Relaxation Techniques and Complete Self-Regulation for Kids to Manage Emotions and Behaviour

By

W. Mumtaz

About the Author

W. Mumtaz is a child psychologist. She is an expert in cognitive-behavioral therapy (CBT) to treat OCD and associated anxiety disorders in children and teenagers. In CBT therapy for anxiety disorders, W. Mumtaz has offered direct patient care and taught child and adolescent therapists and psychologists. She is currently working in a public hospital with special needs children. She has a keen interest in screen-free parenting and child development. She has designed age-appropriate activities for developmental milestones. She is experienced in assessing and devising intervention plans for children's behavioral problems. She is a key public voice teaching children and parents about the fear at the base of anxiety and how it may properly be handled. She is a passionate supporter of the mental health of children and young people.

Table of contents

SELF-REGULATION THROUGH RELAXATION EXERCISES

Introduction

You are reading this book because you are curious if your child has strong emotions. Does your kid start screaming in the supermarket because he insists on taking something you can't let him have? Is your kid constantly getting bored while everyone else appears to be having a great time? Is homework a dreadful experience for your kid? Do you have a hard time teaching your kid?

This book would be for you if you responded yes to any of these concerns.

The behaviors described in the questions above can differ from person to person, but the situation remains the same. These are all signals that your child has some level of emotional dysregulation.

There is one life skill that we must teach our children. But calling it a single skill is a little confusing. It is a collection of abilities. The ability to manage something– a behavior, thinking, an urge, an action, or a feeling. This is called self-regulation. But I also refer to brain control, emotional regulation (management of emotions), and behavioral regulation (control of movements and actions). All of these skills are grouped as self-regulation skills.

Self-regulation relates to dealing with strong emotions such as rage, pleasure, frustration, worry, or depression. Self-control skills can be taught both at home and school. It might be difficult to talk about emotions and determine how someone truly feels. The experience can be motivating and profound in the proper environment with a supporting parent who is calm, loving, and understanding.

The Self-Regulation Workbook for Kids is based on the emotional regulation plan. An emotion regulation plan is an instrument that enables people to acknowledge their emotions, think about why they are experiencing them, and come up with strategies to help them regulate these emotions. These strategies can be especially beneficial for children as their brains develop and learn abilities that will benefit them far into adulthood. Emotion regulation is essential for having healthy interpersonal interactions, positive school or work achievements, and more peaceful existence.

This is not a book about blaming or criticizing others. It is all about growth, transformation, and hope. It motivates you to see how your child can learn to accomplish things in new ways. This will not be simple, and it will necessitate patience and perseverance. With knowledge and application of insight, productive and maladaptive behavior strategies and tactics can be replaced with new, more effective, and adaptable behaviors. Troublesome habits that your kid has developed over time can be altered with calmer, more beneficial interactions.

This book is divided into three parts. Jane, Mia, and Dany are three little kids. They will teach you emotional regulation one by one with different and fun activities. They will tell you about their experiences tips and provide you with all the necessary information that you need to overcome your feelings and thoughts. At the start of each activity, they will tell you basic information. Going further will tell you what to do with the activity, and in the end, expected outcomes are mentioned to help you get a better idea of each activity.

The **first part** focuses on emotions, explaining how they grow, and provides concrete step-by-step strategies that your children may use to deal with damaging and unsettling feelings. This part is mainly about controlling emotions and feelings. With easy and understandable activities, your kid will recognize different emotions connected with the situation. Your kids will enjoy every activity with fun games, interesting worksheets, and engaging questions.

The **second part** employs similar techniques to assist you in reducing the frequency of behavioral outbursts and managing already escalated conduct. This part is all about controlling your thoughts and connecting thoughts with feelings. Our thoughts are responsible for our emotions and behaviors. Eliminating negativity from your kids' lives can make them happier and calmer. That is why I have designed a part on thoughts with fun activities to get your kids' focus towards their negative thoughts so that they can be able to become more positive individuals.

The **third part** tackles your emotional needs by suggesting different exercises to manage your problems. It will provide your kids with fun activities, CBT, and relaxation exercises in easy-to-understand language.

This book is a fantastic instructional resource that covers everything. A short story of three kids that your kids can connect to, lovely drawings that record children's attention, calming-down tasks for kids, directions for grownups on the follow-up exercises, emotional responses cards, thoughts and emotions cards, coloring pages, and related stories to teach kids empathy are all included in the book.

So, what are you waiting for? Ask your kid to join you, and let's get started together.

Importance of Self-Regulation for Strong Emotions

Although we are all created with feelings, not all of them are pre-programmed in our brains. Weeping, disappointment, hunger, and discomfort are all-natural emotional reactions in kids. However, when kids get older, they learn about additional feelings.

There is not much research on which emotions are inborn and learned through emotional, interpersonal, and cultural experiences. Anger, grief, anxiety, joy, surprise, disgust, and humiliation are usually acknowledged as the eight fundamental in-built emotions. These are represented in a variety of ways. Anger, for example, is frequently associated with hatred and aggression, whereas anxiety is frequently associated with fear.

Secondary emotions are inextricably tied to the eight fundamental emotions and represent our emotional responses to certain feelings. These feelings are a result of our life experiences. A kid who has been disciplined for a meltdown, for instance, may feel worried the next time he is upset. When a child has been scolded for showing fear, he may feel ashamed to share the next time when he will be afraid.

Emotional invalidation makes it difficult for children to learn how to manage their emotions. When we teach children to recognize their emotions, we provide them with a framework that allows them to describe how they feel, making it simpler for them to deal with those feelings in a socially acceptable manner.

Emotion management entails more than merely expressing feelings in a socially acceptable manner. It is a three-step approach that includes teaching kids how to recognize emotions, assisting them in identifying what triggers those feelings, and teaching them how to control those emotions on their own.

A kid with weak emotion management abilities throws tantrums all the time, putting the parent-child connection under strain. This can have a detrimental impact on the entire household's atmosphere, including siblings and those around them, and lead to a downward spiral. Similar to friendships, children who cannot control their strong emotions have fewer social abilities. They have a more difficult time developing and maintaining friendships. Anger, disengagement, anxiety, and violent conduct are symptoms of an inability to self-regulate strong emotions.

All of this has the potential to snowball into even more negative consequences: Children who their classmates bully is more likely to drop out of school, engage in delinquent behaviors, abuse substances, and engage in antisocial behaviors. Bullying is more frequent among withdrawn and rejected by their peers.

When we teach children that their feelings are valid, we assist them in seeing their feelings as normal and acceptable. During early life, it is also crucial to set a good example. Showing your child how to respond accordingly to anger is the way to teach them. Children pick up on our emotions, and those exposed to a lot of unpleasant emotions are more likely to have trouble.

Finally, helping children control their emotions begins with acknowledging their feelings and creating a secure setting to express them. Children who feel protected are more likely to learn and employ appropriate emotion control abilities to deal with challenging feelings.

A Message for Grownups

Hey, grownups! The issue is not with the feelings of your children. Adults can understand and respond to their feelings in various ways, but kids cannot. So, as parents, teachers, or concerned adults, how can you be an emotional teacher at a period when children's brains and bodies require the greatest help and practice?

Big emotions can be messy, upsetting, and even overwhelming at times for both children and adults because the area of the brain that helps youngsters deal with emotions is still developing throughout childhood and early adolescence. Emotions can be exceptionally powerful and volatile. As their brains grow, children rely on caring people to help them practice emotional management abilities. We need to be clear on the purpose of teaching so we don't get off track since the emotional journey may get very wild. The goal is not to suffocate or punish strong emotions. The goal is not to raise children who are quiet and obedient.

While you are teaching children about their emotions, you need to understand their emotional responses.

Crying is a natural reaction to being overcome by powerful emotions such as anger, fear, worry, or even joy, at any age. However, some kids cry more than others. Those same children may become enraged more frequently, become frustrated more quickly, and become too thrilled compared to their peers.

The ability to control strong emotions is heavily influenced by age and growth. It is also sometimes just a part of what somebody is to have a more acute experience of things.

Big emotions can make life more challenging for young children unless they learn to regulate their emotions. While this is something that your child will learn on their own, there are some things you can do to assist them in developing emotional awareness and develop healthy coping skills.

Your youngster must be able to understand and articulate their emotions.

Begin teaching children about emotions to understand that even things that appear amorphous or overbearing have a name. Emotional awareness can assist children in being psychologically strong, even while experiencing intense emotions.

But sometimes, parents ignore the emotions of their kids. For example, they respond, "Stop getting so worked up. "It is not a big deal." They instill in the child the belief that their sentiments are incorrect. What you have to do is to put a name to it if you think they are angry, sad, annoyed, ashamed, or disappointed. Then, be empathic and indicate that you understand how they feel.

It is common to have trouble deciding how to respond to extremely emotional kids. It is natural to be puzzled or confused by it all. Even if you do not understand why your child feels the way they do, letting them know that you understand they are going through some feelings and saying that it is OK can be helpful. Feeling "seen" and "embraced" can greatly assist children in learning to recognize, understand, and deal with what they are going through.

With this emotional regulation workbook, you will be able to teach your kids about emotional management, getting rid of their negative thoughts and inner criticism, and helping them practice some easy and fun relaxation exercises. Throughout this workbook, help your kids to complete each activity and keep an eye on your kids' records so that you can better understand what your kid feels.

Hello, Kids!

Hello there, kid. I'm a child psychologist. Every day at my institution, I assist learners with their emotions and moods. It is a crucial component of what I do regularly. This is why I am delighted that you are reading this book to understand your emotions and sentiments better.

The capacity to pay focus, plan and push through, and comprehend emotions are all assisted by self-regulation. We know that you frequently go through different powerful emotional reactions during the day. Helping you to understand emotions and teaching coping methods for dealing with powerful feelings contributes to your mental development.

The more you understand them, the more prepared you'll be to deal with them in various scenarios. You will learn about the major emotions, as well as a variety of other emotions and feelings. You will discover why understanding oneself is so crucial. You will discover everything there is to know about the thoughts in your head that make you frightened or assure you that everything is alright.

Your three new friends are waiting for you. Their names are Jane Mia and Danny, and we will get to meet them in this book. They will help you in your emotional regulation journey. You will discover new ways to manage your feelings and thoughts, as well as how these impact your life. You will also discover how your emotions influence many aspects of your life, such as your relationships and education. But one of the most valuable things you will find in this book is fantastic guidelines and ideas for dealing with sensations that seem overwhelming.

By the time you have finished reading this book, you will have learned so many useful suggestions that you will feel as if you have gained a new superpower, which you surely will.

So, what are you looking for? Start reading and meet your new friends.

PART-I
(Power of Emotions)

My Emotions and Moods

Emotions are an inevitable aspect of life. We face different emotions in our daily life. For instance, when we are caught in traffic, we get annoyed. When we miss our family members, we feel lonely. When someone disappoints us or does us harm, we get angry.

Emotions are simpler to control than moods since they are focused on a single object and do not endure as long. A half-second is all it takes for our brains to recognize an emotional trigger and produce the chemicals that cause an emotional reaction. Moods, on the other side, are impacted by a variety of elements, including the environment (climate, individuals), physiology (food, activity, sleep, disease), thinking (where one's attention is concentrated), and of course, present emotions. Moods might linger for days, whereas emotions only last a few seconds or minutes.

You can tell when you are in a good mood because you are joyful and cheery and when you are in a bad mood, and you are sad and grouchy. Moods differ from emotions in three important ways. To begin with, moods tend to stay considerably longer than emotions, lasting hours or even days, whereas emotions may just last minutes. Second, emotions are focused on a definite subject, such as a person or a circumstance, whereas moods are more unstructured and have no definable target.

Emotions and moods are intertwined. When you are in a bad mood, you are more likely to experience negative feelings like sadness, anger, or fear. However, when you are in a good mood, you are more likely to feel positive feelings like happiness or optimism about something. As a result, the structure of emotions provides insight into the nature of moods.

While we all have times in our lives when our emotional reactions run out of control, some people go through it regularly. Although emotional regulation may seem to be a complex psychological technique, it is a simple mental and behavioral process that many of us are currently involved in, both subconsciously and consciously. Let me use these stories to help you understand your feelings.

STORY TIME

Jane, Mia, and Dany are little kids. They become friends by continuously visiting a psychologist clinic nearby. They live in the same area and go for exercise in the evening with their parents in the same park. Now, they are good friends. Let's listen to their stories.

Jane (13 years old) was rarely in a good mood. He had been bullied as a kid, and his parents did not seem to care about him. He had developed a negative attitude toward himself. Jane's numbness limited his capability to live a fulfilling life.
A psychologist spent some time with him to figure out how he came to feel this way about himself. Jane began to be kinder to himself through time and with practice, and he began to explore healthier ways of expressing his emotions.

Mia (10 years old) was often furious. She had been harmed by those who were supposed to be looking out for her, felt embarrassed of what she was like, and had never learned how to cope. When problems happened, Mia would blame herself, become upset, and frequently react. Mia struggled to perform in her daily life due to her overwhelming emotions.
The psychologist assisted her in recognizing why she was so angry. They looked at some options, and Mia discovered coping methods for her intense emotions.

Dany (11 years old) struggled with anxiety. He felt his heart pounding the inside of his chest. He made every effort to avoid situations where he had previously panicked and felt uncomfortable whenever he had to go somewhere new. Dany was experiencing too much fear, which was negatively harming his life. He had a conversation with a psychologist. She aided Dany by recommending certain activities and requested him to write down everything he encountered in different scenarios. Dany became less afraid of his body and its responses, and he could confront the things that had earlier terrified him.

I have asked Jane, Mia, and Dany to help you by teaching you the key activities and exercises they learned and experienced during their emotional regulation journey. So, Let's go...

ACTIVITY - All About Me

Before we start, Jane, Mia and Dany want to know about you. Fill this to let them know about your favorites.

1. Hello! My name is _____.
2. I am _____ years old.
3. I was born on _____.
4. I live in _____.
5. My mother is a _____ and father is a _____.
6. My family members are _____.
7. I want to be _____.
8. I like _____ to do for fun
9. My favorite subject is _____.
10. My favorite place is _____.
11. I like to go to_____.
12. In my free time, I like to _____.
13. I am good at _____.
14. I like to watch _____.
15. I am not good at _____.
16. My favorite food is _____.

One Interesting Story About Me

_____

_____

_____

_____

_____

_____

ACTIVITY- <u>The Way I Feel</u>

Hi! I am Jane. I will share my recovery journey to help you get out of your emotional problems. When I visited my psychologist, she asked me to write down what I felt, and the situation around me made me feel that emotion. Follow me. I will teach you how to do this.

What to Do: Think of yourself and your emotions. How do you feel in a certain situation, and what makes you feel like that? Think, draw your emotions in the circles and write any two most common reasons in one word that you can think of.

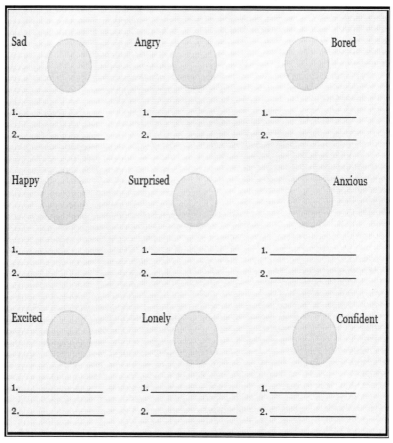

Expected Outcomes: Kids will recognize their triggers for the most commonly prevalent emotions.

ACTIVITY- <u>My Worry Box</u>

What to Do: I am Mia, and it is my turn. Friend, you are not alone. We all face some difficulties in our life, and even grown-ups also face these emotions. I am going to give you a worry box. So, every time you feel overwhelmed or worried, come to me, write your worry in this box and put a cage over it so it cannot get out to make you worry again. Make sure when you put the cage on your worry, give a smile.

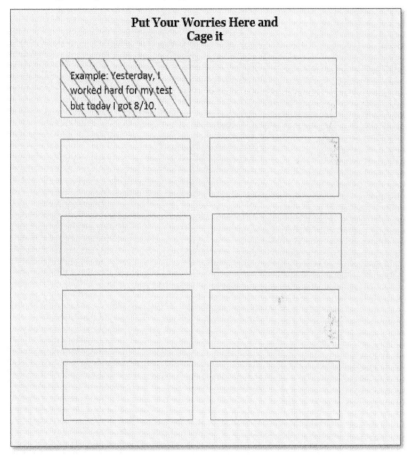

Expected Outcomes: You will be able to get out of your worries through this fun activity. Kids will learn to let go of their bad days fast. They will get one step closer to a fulfilling life.

ACTIVITY- <u>My Stress Jar</u>

Hey kid! Dany here. Do you know stress jars are a must-have when you have difficulty with your emotions? I am sharing the recipe to fill out your stress jar to empty your mind with all the situations that cause it.

What to do: There is a jar in front of you. You just have to color the emotions in the jar. I am giving you three levels of your stress. Suppose you feel normal stress, e.g., for your math test, color the emotion yellow. If it is more than usual, e.g., you are going to a party and stress about being noticed for your clothes, color it blue, and if it is high, it affects your physical movements, e.g., butterflies in the stomach, color it red. After filling the jar, count the emotions with the same color and write the results at the top of your stress jar.

Normal	High	Extreme
Yellow	Blue	Red

Expected Outcomes: These jars teach kids to comfort themselves, settle down, breathe deeply, and deal with their problems safely and productively.

ACTIVITY- <u>My Emotional Stages</u>

Jane: Now it is time to understand your emotional stages to regulate these. There will be five words, and you have to write something about each word.

What to do: There are five words given below. Think of a story related to the word and write in the given space. The story must be related to you, which had a huge impact on your life.

Rejection (You have been rejected by someone or somewhere)

_____

_____

_____

_____

_____

_____

_____

Depressed (Situation happened and you became depressed)

_____

_____

_____

_____

_____

_____

_____

Angry (Situation happened and you became really angry)

_____

_____

_____

_____

_____

_____

_____

Emotional (Situation happened, and you felt emotional at that time)

_____

_____

_____

_____

_____

_____

_____

Acceptance (Situation happened, and you accepted it as it was)

_____

_____

_____

_____

_____

_____

_____

Expected Outcomes: This will assist your children in processing their loss by allowing them to consider how they have responded to each of the five stages of emotions. If your child gets stuck at one of the stages, push them to go deeply into it and listen to their story.

ACTIVITY- <u>My Emotions and Actions</u>

Mia: Jane has taught you about your five emotional stages. I am helping you to keep a record of your actions during a certain emotional situation. When I visited my psychologist, she gave me a sheet and asked me to keep updating my reactions whenever I passed through an event that caused different emotions. I am sharing the same sheet with you.

What to do: Here is a worksheet below. You need to write your emotion, the situation that happened, and how you reacted to that emotion. For example, I was angry about not having my favorite food, and I reacted by shouting or skipping my dinner. In this example, being angry is your emotion, not having favorite food is the situation and shouting loudly/skipping dinner is a reaction. In the last column, write whether your reaction was good or bad.

My Actions and Reactions Diary			
My Emotions	**What Happened?**	**My Reaction**	**Good or Bad**

Expected Outcomes: When kids are honest about their emotions, they can better control them. Writing emotions and their reactions allows them to understand their actions and control their mental wellbeing.

ACTIVITY- <u>My Positive Emotions</u>

Dany: Jane and Mia have done a good job teaching you about your emotions and how you react in a certain situation. But I think it is really important to know your positive emotions and what causes you to feel positive. So, I want to know more about you being positive before going further.

<u>What to do</u>: A list of positive emotions is prepared for you. You have to write what made you feel this way. You can write as many situations as you think of.

<u>My Positive Emotions Diary</u>	
<u>Happy</u>	
<u>Calm</u>	
<u>Lucky</u>	
<u>Confident</u>	

Excited	
Brave	
Peaceful	
Awesome	

Expected Outcomes: Your kid will learn to pay more attention to his positive expressions and will be able to appreciate positivity in his life. Whenever he thinks of a positive situation, he will become happier.

ACTIVITY- <u>Emotions Daily Check-In</u>

Jane, Mia, and Dany want you to record your emotions daily in the next activity. Do not skip a day and see how you feel most of your time.

<u>**What to do**</u>: This worksheet consists of days of the week and Morning, Afternoon, and Evening times. You need to draw or write the emotion during the whole time. It can be one, two, or more. So, be honest with yourself.

My Daily Emotions Diary			
<u>**Days**</u>	<u>**Morning**</u> 6:00-11:00 a.m.	<u>**Noon/Afternoon**</u> 12:00-5:00 p.m.	<u>**Evening/Night**</u> 5:00-11:00 p.m.
Monday			
Tuesday			
Wednesday			
Thursday			
Friday			
Saturday			
Sunday			

Monday			
Tuesday			
Wednesday			
Thursday			
Friday			
Saturday			
Sunday			

Expected Outcomes: Daily check-in of the emotions are an open-ended method for children to express emotions on paper that may be too confused to express in their minds alone. Your kids will analyze their thoughts while also sorting through negative emotions. This will also help kids comprehend why they feel the way they do and allow them to consider alternative viewpoints.

ACTIVITY- <u>My Mood Zones</u>

Jane: In all the previous activities, we asked you about your emotions in a specific situation and how you felt, reacted, and responded. Now, I want you to tell me which emotion zone you have built in your mind.

What to do: Here, I have given you four zones that are blue, green, yellow, and red. I have also given some emotions at the end. You have to put that emotion in a zone where you feel that emotion belongs. You can only use one emotion under one zone. I have given an example to understand what type of emotion can be put in which zone.

My Zone of Emotions			
Blue	**Green**	**Yellow**	**Red**
Sad	Happy	Frustrated	Angry

Emotions: Sad, Mad, Angry, Hitting, Wiggly, Excited, Feeling Okay, Focused, Tired, Elated, Bored, Frustrated, Calm, Yelling, Happy, Out of Control, Ready to Learn, Sick, Moving Slowly, Worried, Silly, Loss of Some Control

Expected Outcomes: Creating a personal emotional zone will help your kid to understand the emotions that are normal, emotions that are Ok for some time, and emotions that are harmful to mental wellbeing.

ACTIVITY- <u>My Calming Strategy</u>

Mia: As we grow up, we make judgments, hopes, ambitions, and rules for ourselves and our lives. Same as, when we feel different emotions from time to time, we also make some strategies for ourselves that make us calm right after we feel a certain emotion. For example, when I struggled with my emotions, I quickly became angry. So, I made a strategy that I would drink a glass of water whenever I became angry.

<u>What to do</u>: First of all, I have a question for you. You need to answer it honestly about it. Then I am giving you some very easy tasks. You have to do it by yourself, with your parents or friends and mark in the last column if it helped you to calm down or not at all.

Question: What is your calming strategy whenever you feel certain emotion?

_____

_____

_____

_____

_____

_____

(It is alright if you don't have any, leave this blank and whenever you find out your strategy, fill this at that time.)

To Do's	Yes	No	Little Bit
Read something funny.			
Think that someone cares about you.			
Talk about you with someone closer.			

Ask for help in difficulty.			
Color your cartoon hero.			
Play Puzzles.			
Do some exercise.			
Listen to music.			
Take a walk with your near one.			
Put some lotion on your feet.			
Play with your pet.			
Have some snacks.			
Eat your favorite dish.			
Go for shopping.			
Take a shower.			
Recall ABC backward.			
Draw different cartoons.			
Take deep breaths.			
Blow five candles.			
Count the stairs.			
Jump seven times.			
Play hide and seek with your friends.			
Look in the mirror for 10 minutes.			

Close your eyes and imagine yourself in your dream place.			
Play with a ball.			
Hug someone for 2 minutes.			
Stand in front of the mirror and make five different faces.			

Expected Outcomes: Use this sheet as your kid's calm down strategy whenever he feels angry or frustrated. Your kid will love to do these things, and instead of taking exercises as a part of learning, he will take it as fun.

ACTIVITY- <u>My Strengths</u>

<u>*Dany*</u>: Do you know that you have many things you are good at, you can do many good things, and you are stronger in your way. But sometimes, due to our weaknesses, we can't see our strengths. We always think that we are weaker in this specific thing and we cannot do this thing, etc. So, here I want you to know about your strengths and admire your positives as well.

<u>What to do</u>: Below is the worksheet that you need to answer. This worksheet consists of 1 statement asking you possible answers. Think and answer.

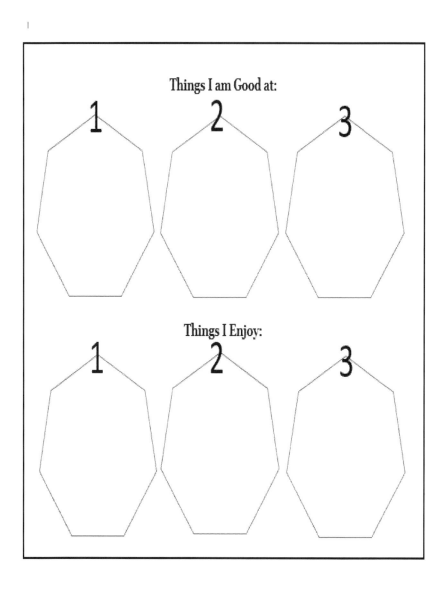

Things I am Good at:

Things I Enjoy:

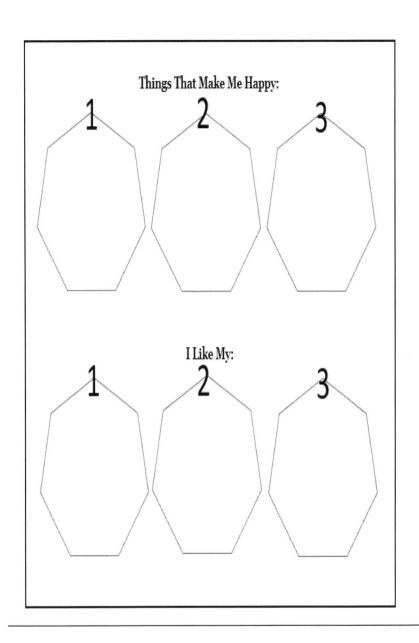

Things That Make Me Happy:

I Like My:

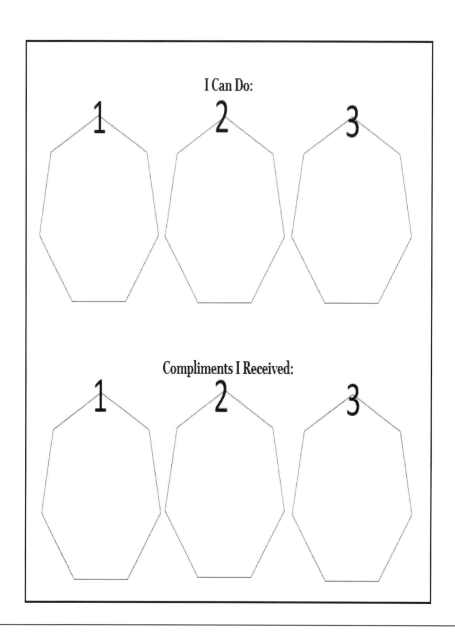

I Can Do:

1   2   3

Compliments I Received:

1   2   3

Expected Outcomes: Through this worksheet, your kids will be able to boost their wellbeing and develop key skills to support them at hard times and into their future. This will also help you (parents) connect with your kids to know about their mental health and life goals.

ACTIVITY- My Weaknesses

***Jane*:** Accepting your weaknesses is also as important as appreciating your strengths. No one is born perfect. We all face some issues with different things, and even grown-ups also can't do many things. So, do not lose hope. You do not have to set back due to your weaknesses. Do not let your weakness disturb your happy life. Use this activity as a tool for the acceptance of your weaknesses.

What to do: Below is the worksheet that you need to answer. This worksheet consists of 1 statement asking you possible answers. Think and answer.

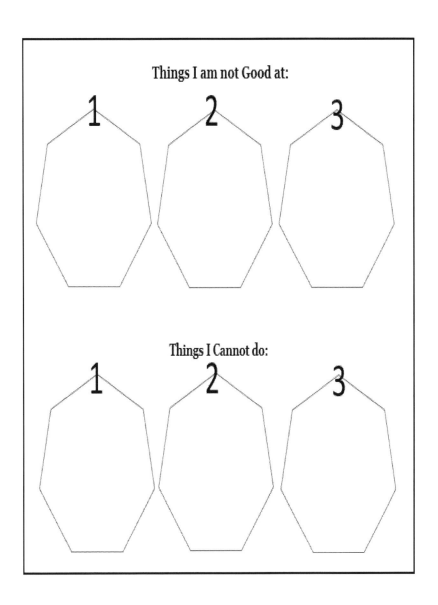

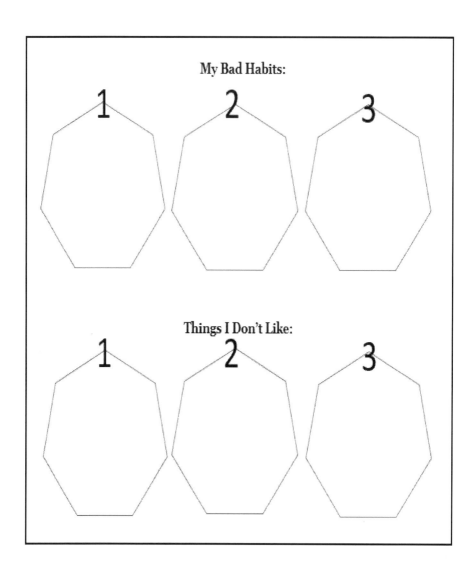

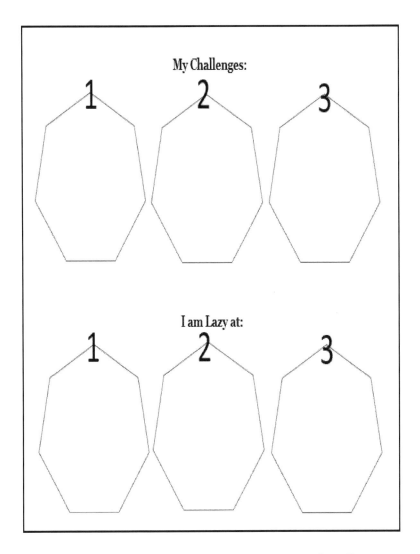

Expected Outcomes: Knowing your strengths allows you to set higher goals and achieve much more. Knowing about their weaknesses, your kid will be able to understand better what may be holding them back, and they can also find ways to avoid the weaknesses that are dragging them down.

ACTIVITY- <u>I am Unique</u>

<u>*Mia:*</u> We are all different with different talents and abilities. These talents and abilities make us special in many ways. I am unique because I can dance well at this age. My dance teacher always appreciates me in the whole class, and I feel special whenever she compliments me. I want you to write down some of your abilities and talents that make you special in your friends, class, or house.

<u>**What to do**</u>: There, I have given you several statements. Please read them carefully and answer in words only.

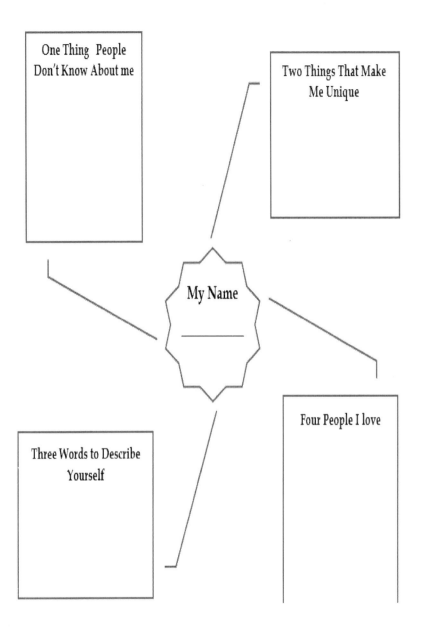

One Thing People Don't Know About me

Two Things That Make Me Unique

My Name

_____

Three Words to Describe Yourself

Four People I love

Expected Outcomes: You should recognize that you are different from others to feel unique. No one else is perfectly like you. This individuality arises from within, as shown by our acts and behaviors. Doing this activity will allow your kids to think of themselves as one of a kind. They will see their worth and that they are not ordinary human beings. They are different in their way.

GAME- <u>My Feelings Puzzle</u>

Dany: So much to do but not having fun? Don't be upset about it. Jane and Mia helped me to prepare a game for you to be able to relax a bit.

<u>What to do</u>: This puzzle consists of different emotions. Find out these emotions. Draw that emotion in a space next to the word below the puzzle. Keep in mind you are only allowed to draw that emotion when you find that emotion in the puzzle. We have given you a list of emotions that you need to find in the puzzle for your help. I have done one for you.

```
d H d C D y G s R h Q q j f B v R w U y
e e a e r L u s y y K f d f J d w q p p
F l s C s o o V t S l e e p y g g p o S
m F K u v s h v S a d k E C Y M a z i d
H f L r f a a I e N T c K h w H a l F e
C Q e C F n o r I d v i j i N i l d r t
G N q E T d o u r f U S D n n y v Z u n
N s C B q o M C w a y h s f Z d w M s i
M x y r g n A T O F b u z b F t D X t o
C J z D b f l X v d X m T Z p y G p r p
W n B I x R Y Y P F N e E Z O X J w a p
P B g h F c N q S u r p r i s e d A t a
W K L n G E H X a d p J l j a z C m e s
U t i G j x P F y E t v w v h b S a d i
F L X H f c u N P Q t f b g C Z V z U D
X z U w Q i K D P T K C s N l R G e N t
K D M U L t T L N A o G a j z o j d L F
X v G G M e B G E T I J M I B i T S L p
o j T U u d H C F t F H I X G B x V C N
b m p L n R S M o T w d q E v m g m d w
```

Happy _____ 😊

Sad	Mad	Excited	Calm
___	___	___	___

Shy	Confused	Sick	Cry
___	___	___	___

Surprised	Loved	Amazed	Silly
___	___	___	___

Angry	Embarrassed	Disappointed	Nervous
___	___	___	___

Sleepy	Kind	Frustrated
___	___	___

Expected Outcome: The purpose of this fun game is to help your kids relax and keep their focus on emotional regulation activities. They will also be able to work on their tolerance and knowledge.

ACTIVITY- <u>I Can Manage</u>

Jane, Mia, Dany: You are strong. Whatever will be the situation, you can manage it. You can handle it. Don't be sad, worried, or lose hope. You can achieve everything with your hard work. You just have to put your heart into it and let the magic happen. We have prepared a list of tasks that can teach you how to manage your situations. When we struggled with emotions like you, we gave our best to these little tasks, and the result amazed us. We started managing all situations, no matter how big or small they were. We want you to try all these tasks before going on the next journey.

<u>What to do</u>: Here is the list of some easy tasks. You need to do something related to the task and write how it helped you in your daily life in the result section. For example, if the task is time management, you need to manage your everyday work with time. Like I chose to make a study schedule to manage time. The study schedule helped me regulate my study, and my grades improved little by little as a result. It is your turn now.

Tasks	How You Managed	Result in Everyday Life
Time Management		
Resources (Money, Food) Management		
Mood Management		
Anger		

Management		
Emotions Management		
Health Management		
Thoughts Management		
Decision Making Management		

Expected Outcomes: This management practice can assist your children in recognizing and comprehending their emotions, as well as explaining why they might be so intense at times. It provides some practical suggestions for how they might handle their major life events to use and manage them while being independent of them.

(If kids find it difficult to do, you (parents) can help them in managing tasks)

PART-II
(My CBT Guide)

How does CBT Work?

CBT (Cognitive Behavior Therapy) is a psychological treatment useful for various concerns, including anxiety, emotional problems, alcohol and drug abuse issues, marital issues, eating disorders, and serious mental disease. According to numerous research studies, CBT improves performance and quality of life significantly.

CBT is built on the concept that your thinking, feelings, and behaviors are interconnected. To put it another way, how you think or feel about something might impact what you do. For instance, if you are stressed out at work, you can perceive things differently and make decisions you wouldn't normally make. However, another important CBT idea is that these thinking and behavior patterns can be changed.

CBT focuses on assisting individuals in becoming their own therapists. Patients/clients are assisted in developing coping skills through exercises in the meeting and "homework" assignments outside of sessions, allowing them to learn to alter their thoughts, negative emotions, and behavior.

CBT therapists focus on the person's current situation rather than the events that led to their problems. Although some information about one's past is required, the focus is generally on moving forward in time to develop more effective coping skills.

CBT is among the most investigated types of therapy. Many specialists believe that it is the most effective treatment for various mental health issues. CBT can be beneficial. However, there are a few points to bear in mind if you decide to try this. Therapy can help you cope with your problems, but it won't necessarily solve them. Therapy can be emotionally exhausting. It can help you improve over time, but the process might be challenging.

But you don't need to worry. I hope Jane, Mia, and Dany are your friends now. They will not leave you in between. They are once again here to help you recognize and change your thoughts. This time, they will talk less and provide you with more information about each activity and how it affects you. You need to listen to them and fill out each activity carefully. They have worked hard for you by making and organizing these easy and fun activities. Don't give up but try hard until you achieve positive results.

ACTIVITY- <u>My Helping Thoughts</u>

Jane: Sometimes, many of our thoughts help us in a certain situation. Our thoughts make us happy. We love thinking about many things and laughing inside. These thoughts are important for our mental well-being. For example, thinking about having a grand birthday party will make me happiest. Thinking about spending a whole day in an amusement park with my friends will also make me excited. These are all helping thoughts.

<u>What to do</u>: Think of the things you love to do or what you want to do in your life to find out your helping thoughts. Write down on the leaves below (tree leaves) and let that tree have more leaves if you need to write more.

Expected Outcomes: Positive thinking can help your kids manage their stress and possibly enhance their health as effective stress management is linked to the many health advantages. When your child recognizes his helping thoughts, he will be aware of what matters in his life and what things make him happier.

ACTIVITY- <u>My Hurting Thoughts</u>

<u>***Mia***</u>*:* Often, we think negatively about a situation or event that has happened or going to happen. When we think negatively, we indulge in our negative thoughts, and we start thinking about all the things negatively. Thinking negatively ruins our mood and our inner self, our positivity, and in the end, our happy life.

<u>**What to do**</u>: Think of your negative thoughts that hurt you. Outline the leaf that you think is going to fall first. Write your hurtful thought on that leaf and draw your emotion inside the leaf. Be happy after writing because the leaf will fall soon, and the same as the hurtful thought will leave your body soon. If you want to color, color the leaves yellow and orange.

ACTIVITY- <u>Self-Talk</u>

Dany: The unending stream of unsaid thoughts that go through your head is known as self-talk. These thoughts might be either positive or negative. Logic and reason play a role in some of your self-talk. Other self-talk may result from misunderstandings you acquire as a result of a lack of knowledge. If most of your thoughts are negative, you are more likely to have a negative attitude toward life.

<u>What to do</u>: Here, I have an apple tree for you. Write the positive thought you had with yourself in a whole day in an apple. Color the apple red if it made you happier. Color the apple light green if it made you less happy.

Expected Outcomes: Self-talk is a common starting point for positive thinking. When your kid starts to have positive self-talk, he will be more likely to be more optimistic. He will focus more on his positive thinking and let go of his negative mindset.

ACTIVITY- <u>My Choice: Ignore or Listen</u>

Jane: In some ways, ignoring our thoughts is a good thing. We have a lot of work ahead of us. Our lives are filled with tasks, upkeep, and thoughts that need to be considered. But keep in mind that you just have to ignore your negative thoughts. When you recognize that this thought is harmful to your mental health, you will be more likely to ignore that thought easily. To recognize your negative thoughts, I have a worksheet for you.

What to do: Whatever comes to your mind about a specific situation or event, write it down here. After an hour, open this worksheet again. Select the option if you should have ignored or listened to this thought in the future. Set your mind accordingly and stick to it.

My Thoughts	I Should Ignore	I Should Listen

Expected Outcomes: Writing down all thoughts and choosing after some time about ignoring or listening is a great way for your kid to understand the importance of that thought in his life. Doing this, again and again, will teach him to recognize his negative thought right after he has them. By that time, your kid will have a more positive mindset.

ACTIVITY- <u>Catching My Thoughts</u>

Mia: Before thoughts can be analyzed or questioned, they must first be 'caught' or separated from events and experiences. The Catching Thoughts worksheet is meant to help kids practice recognizing and recording their automatic thoughts and recognizing triggering circumstances and emotional responses.

<u>What to do</u>: Do you have a thought? Write the situation about what happened or what made you have that thought. Write the feeling you are having. Then write about the thought that you had. I have written one example for you.

Situation	Feelings	Thoughts
I broke a glass jar.	Upset and scared	Mom will scold me.

Expected Outcomes: Thoughts are broad statements that influence how a person perceives himself, other people, and reality. These are defined as a set of beliefs that govern behavior in a variety of settings. Although automatic thoughts are not facts, we often believe them to be true because they are quick and familiar. This worksheet will assist your kids in honing their skills in recognizing and recording automatic thoughts and recognizing triggering situations and the emotional reactions that follow them.

ACTIVITY- <u>My Thinking Errors</u>

<u>Dany</u>: What are the most common thinking errors we make by indulging in our thoughts? Hey kid! Do you know that we pay greater attention to negative events and neglect positive events? Without adequate knowledge, we believe we know what somebody is thinking or why they are doing something. We believe that we know what will happen in the future and be unpleasant. The only way to stop these thoughts is to highlight them first.

<u>What to do</u>: Here, some kids are in a bad mood and talking about their thoughts. The only problem is that they ignore the positive and only focus on the negative. For example, the boy is crying because he has got one answer wrong in a mathematics test. But what about the right ones? He is ignoring the truth that he has got nine correct answers. The only thing he cares about is the wrong answer. Just look at the picture, see how they think negatively, and observe the situation.

Expected Outcomes: Kids pay greater attention to stories and other kids like them. The observation activity will help them identify their thinking errors through the life events of other kids. They will be able to restructure their thoughts by observing similar examples.

ACTIVITY- <u>Voice of Truth</u>

Jane: When we face a situation in our life, we make some assumptions. We think negatively and much more. But where is the truth? We don't care about the reality of the situation, and we just focus on all the negative stuff. For example, the teacher asks you to come to the staff room. You think that she will scold you or want to ask something that will embarrass you in front of other teachers. But the reality could be different. May be teacher wants to see you in the staff room because he has a task for you. So, the voice of truth is important before having any thought in your mind.

<u>What to do</u>: In the picture below, thoughts clouds have been given. Write down the negative thought you had in a situation or event. Then write the truth that happened and was the opposite of your thought.

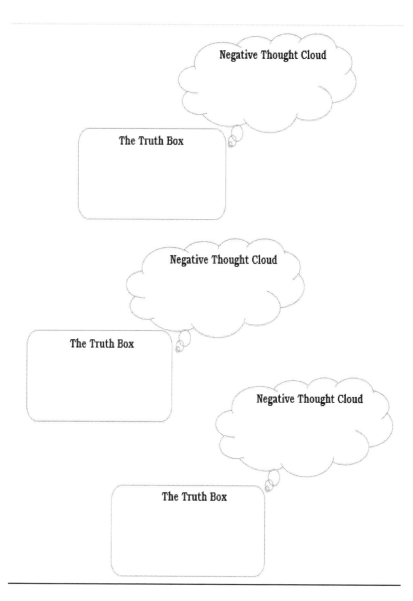

Expected Outcomes: Knowing that a situation could have positivity helped your kid go forward to a positive lifestyle is extremely helpful. He will be able to keep in mind the positive thought before having any negative thoughts about a situation, and eventually, he will start having positive thoughts that will lead him to seek the real truth.

ACTIVITY- <u>Changing Anxiousness into Useful Thinking</u>

<u>Mia</u>: When we have negative thoughts, some thoughts turn into anxious thoughts, leading us to be stressed and depressed. They could last for a longer period. We think about them repeatedly, and in the end, we become sleep-deprived because of those anxious thoughts. But there is a way out of these anxious thoughts. For this, you need to get out of your negativity zone, and then you would be able to change your anxiousness into useful thinking.

<u>What to do</u>: Here I have a worksheet for you. Write about a thought that you think made you feel stressed and anxious. Change it into useful thinking that will motivate you. I have written an example for you.

My Anxious Thoughts	Changing into Useful Thinking
I have always stood first in my class, but I have got the second position this time. I am not a good student anymore.	I have got the second position in the class. This must be because I haven't work hard. I should focus on my studies more.

Expected Outcomes: Having useful thoughts will help your kids learn and grow more in different areas of life. This is an important part of being a positive person that you must have the skill to change your negativity into usefulness. A successful and happier person only thinks about useful stuff that helps him grow faster and better. This activity is a great tool for your kids' learning.

ACTIVITY- <u>Creating Happiness</u>

Dany: We live in a world where many thoughts come into our minds with a lot of stuff happening around us. But we need to ignore the negative and find our happiness by ourselves. Our happiness comes with our positive mindset. Think of the things that make you happy and make yourself the happiest person.

<u>What to do</u>: You are the kid with the thoughts cloud in the picture below. These thought clouds are empty because you need to write your source of happiness. Think, write and color the clouds before they fly far away from you.

Expected Outcomes: The purpose of this activity is to make your kid happy by thinking about the stuff he likes to do. This will also help you find out what your kid likes to do and his thoughts about having a happy life.

ACTIVITY- <u>Getting Rid of Negativity</u>

Jane: You have learned to recognize and change your negative thoughts. But this is not the end of negativity. You must have eliminated it from your life. You want to be a happy person. For this, you should get rid of all your negative thoughts. But how? Friend! Don't worry. I am sharing positivity stairs with you that helped me a lot during my journey of becoming a positive person.

What to do: Start with the upper stair. The upper stair shows the level of negativity you have. Come down by following the rules on each stair. Once you have followed the first rule, come down to second and then next and next. In the end, after following each rule, you will reach the land, which is called the land of positivity.

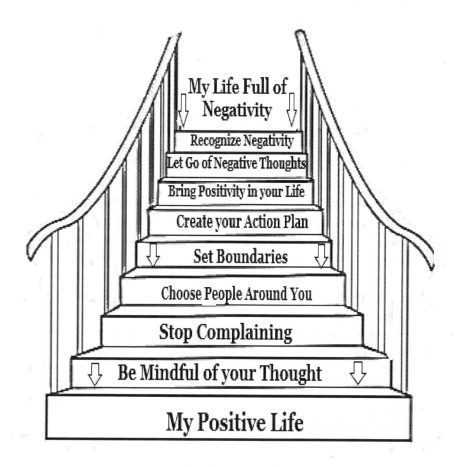

Expected Outcomes: These rules are called golden rules for having a positive lifestyle. By following these rules, your kid will have better mental wellbeing. You will see clear changes in the thoughts and actions of your kid. If kids feel hard to follow these rules, help them out but don't skip a single stair.

ACTIVITY- <u>Challenging Negative Thoughts</u>

<u>**Mia**</u>: Have you started following golden rules for positive life? With these rules, you have to challenge your negative thoughts whenever they pop up in your mind. Above, you changed your thoughts into useful thinking, but now you have to alter your thoughts into positive ones completely. For example, "I hate this artwork." This is a negative thought. But you can change it into positive thoughts like, "This artwork must have a story behind it. I should try to focus more on the details." Easy? Let's try this.

<u>**What to do**</u>: Write the negative thought that you are having about an event or situation. Change it to a positive one by focusing inner truth of the scenario.

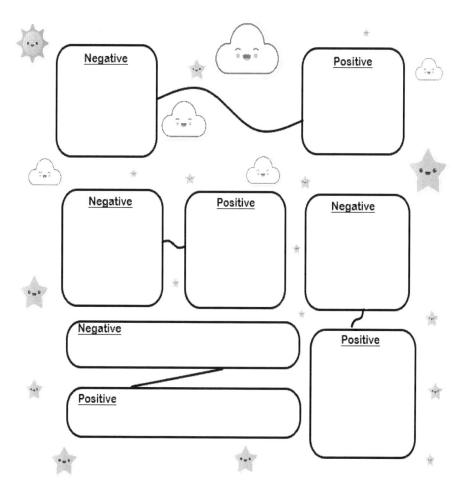

Expected Outcomes: Changing negativity into positivity is a difficult task, but it can be achievable by practicing again and again. This activity will assist your kids in learning changing the scenarios for making a thought positive. Kids will also learn to have a different perspective on things they don't like.

ACTIVITY- <u>Think and Feel</u>

Dany: This activity combines your feelings and thoughts, so you don't forget what you have learned in the first part. You just need to link your thoughts with your emotions by using single words. You can do it. Right?

<u>**What to do**</u>: In the picture below, you need to think about what makes you feel the emotions described in each shape. For example, when I think about taking a pool bath, I feel embarrassed. Write in a word and color the shapes.

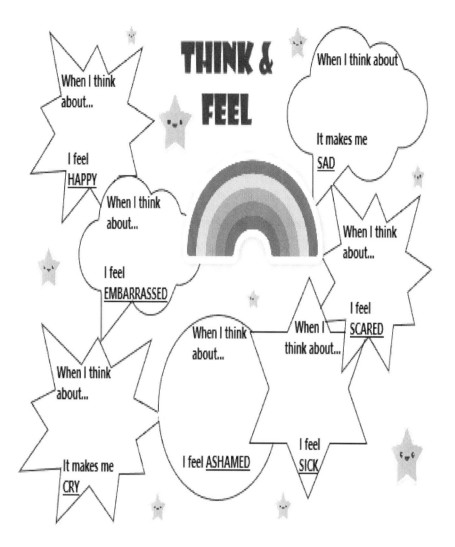

THINK & FEEL

When I think about...
I feel HAPPY

When I think about...
It makes me SAD

When I think about...
I feel EMBARRASSED

When I think about...
I feel SCARED

When I think about...

When I think about...
I feel ASHAMED

When I think about...
I feel SICK

When I think about...
It makes me CRY

Expected Outcomes: This is a simple activity to make your kids learn that their thoughts are linked with their emotions. Whatever they think, the thought will automatically change their feelings and emotions. For example, if they have a happy thought, they will smile or laugh.

ACTIVITY- <u>Thoughts Record Worksheet</u>

Jane, **_Mia_**, **and** **_Dany_**: In the first part, we gave you a daily emotions record worksheet. Here we are giving you daily thoughts record worksheet. We want to see the progress that you have made day by day. This worksheet will also help you observe your thoughts for a whole day. Be careful not to miss a single day.

<u>What to do</u>: Come and fill the boxes with your thoughts during that time. These could be one or more. Write all and before going to bed, observe your day.

Days	Morning Thoughts	Noon/Afternoon Thoughts	Night Thoughts
Monday			
Tuesday			
Wednesday			
Thursday			
Friday			
Saturday			
Sunday			

Monday			
Tuesday			
Wednesday			
Thursday			
Friday			
Saturday			
Sunday			

Expected Outcomes: This worksheet will help you and your kids be updated about the progress and the thoughts that kids had during a whole day. You will help him out if your kid is having a hard day. Keep an eye on the sheet and help your kid get out of his negative thoughts.

ACTIVITY- <u>Fighting my Inner Critic</u>

<u>Jane</u>, ***<u>Mia</u>***, **and** ***<u>Dany</u>***: Inner criticism could become downright self-destructive because your negative thoughts have such a strong influence on how you feel and act. Telling yourself that you will never be successful or that you are not as excellent as other people lower your self-esteem and prevent you from confronting your anxieties. You are not alone if you tend to be overly critical of yourself. Self-doubt and severe self-reflection are common experiences for most people. You do not have to be a target of your verbal abuse. Rather, take proactive actions to address your inner critic. Fighting inner criticism is as important as changing negative thoughts into positive ones. But we will help you.

<u>What to do</u>: Find out the inner critic you have made about yourself. Write it as a judgment box. Change it into a positive sentence, and write it into the fighting box. For example, my inner critic is, "I will never be a successful person in my life". I will fight back by changing the sentence to "If I work hard, I will be a successful person" one day.

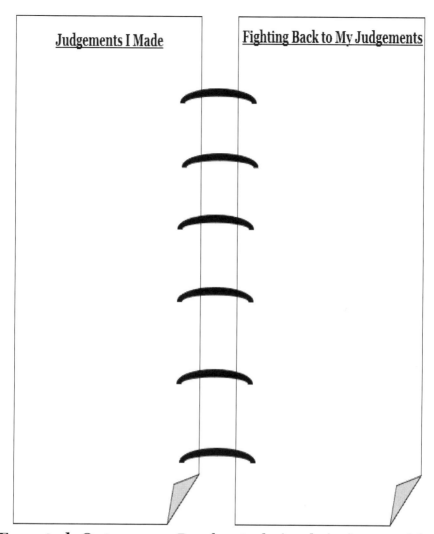

Judgements I Made

Fighting Back to My Judgements

Expected Outcomes: People stuck in their inner critic become unaware of their negative thoughts. They tend to criticize themselves and become self-destructive. By doing this activity, your kids will know what inner critic is and what limits they create when they self-critic. Help your kids to find out their inner critics so that they can live a more fulfilling life.

PART-III

(My Management Pack)

Why is Self-Regulation Important?

Emotional regulation is a deeply personal process. Some people are taught strong coping abilities, while others are given little to no behavioral advice as youngsters. Still, emotional control is a talent that can be learned and developed with practice, just like any other ability. Meditation, along with breathing techniques and self-awareness measures, are one of the various treatments for some people.

Strong emotional regulation abilities may increase long-term wellbeing, boost professional performance, enrich personal relations, and even contribute to better general health, in addition to the clearer advantages, such as feeling better in the short term.

Furthermore, self-managing emotions by problem-solving, expressing oneself, reconsidering the circumstance, and other methods reduces the likelihood of those emotions escalating and leading to undesirable outcomes. While moods are not the same as emotions, emotions certainly impact our moods. This indicates that emotional management can lead to improved mood, leading to more empathy and compassion for others in the long term.

Emotional regulation is not a natural ability. The mood of a kid may swing like a wave. One of the most crucial responsibilities for parents is to help their children self-regulate various emotions. This part will teach you about self-regulation and how activities and exercises help kids develop this important ability.

Learning to self-regulate is a critical milestone in a child's development, with roots returning to birth. The ability of a kid to control their emotional state and reactions impacts their family, peers, academic success, long-term mental health, and ability to survive in a complicated environment. So, it is really important to learn how to self-regulate our emotions to make our life more fulfilling.

However, anyone who wants to enhance their emotional control abilities should not be ashamed of unpleasant or undesired feelings. Everyone has them; what matters is what we do with them.

So, you don't have to be worried; we (Jane, Mia, and Dany) are again here to help you with your self-regulation strategies and exercises.

Self-Regulation through Fun Activities (Individual)

FUN ACTIVITY- <u>Make a "Feelings Bank"</u>

***Jane*:** Nice to meet you again, friends. I am wondering how would be your overall journey with us. I hope we have helped you with your emotional struggles. Now we will give you some fun activities and exercises to keep yourself relaxed and stress-free. Start with the simplest one. Here I have a worksheet for you to collect your feelings.

<u>What to do</u>: Write out every emotion you can recall that you ever felt on a quiet morning. No feeling should go unnoticed, especially if it is something you are not used to discussing. <u>Parents of teenagers, take note:</u> Have your child write down all of the bodily experiences that they connect with each emotion next to it. Hang this checklist somewhere. They will see it often, such as on their wardrobe door or by their mirror. Return to the list several times over a day or week to add to it. Because performing this all at once can often lead to overload, I recommend doing it over some time.

My Emotions	Bodily Experience Connected with the Emotion

Expected Outcomes: With this simplest activity, your kids will learn to observe their feelings and how their body reactions change with their emotions, thoughts, and actions. They will overcome the negativity by discovering that it is harmful to their body reactions.

FUN ACTIVITY- Mood Meter

Mia: On the inside, how you are feeling can have a big impact on how you behave on the outside. Our emotions have a major influence on our decision-making, but we are often unaware of how we are feeling or how those emotions are affecting our behaviors at the moment. Don't worry because I have Mood Meter for you. It is a square split into 4 quadrants, each reflecting a different set of emotions: red (on the upper left), blue (on the lower left), yellow (on the upper right), and green (on the lower right). Different moods are grouped depending on their pleasantness (in rows) and energy level (in columns) on the Mood Meter.

What to do: Before you plan to do something (going on a walk, for instance), check on the mood meter about which color zone you fall in. If it is red or blue (feeling depressed or sad), you need to do something to come into the green or yellow zone. Make a plan that will boost your energy level. Color the zones red, yellow, blue, and green as described above for your easiness.

Enraged	Panicked	Stressed	Jittery	Shocked		Surprised	Upbeat	Festive	Exhilarated	Ecstatic
Livid	Furious	Frustrated	Tense	Stunned		Hyper	Cheerful	Motivated	Inspired	Elated
Fuming	Frightened	Angry	Nervous	Restless		Energized	Lively	Excited	Optimistic	Enthusiastic
Anxious	Apprehensive	Worried	Irritated	Annoyed		Pleased	Focused	Happy	Proud	Thrilled
Repulsed	Troubled	Concerned	Uneasy	Peeved		Pleasant	Joyful	Hopeful	Playful	Blissful

Disgusted	Glum	Disappointed	Down	Apathetic		At Ease	Easygoing	Content	Loving	Fulfilled
Pessimistic	Morose	Discouraged	Sad	Bored		Calm	Secure	Satisfied	Grateful	Touched
Alienated	Miserable	Lonely	Disheartened	Tired		Relaxed	Chill	Restful	Blessed	Balanced
Despondent	Depressed	Sullen	Exhausted	Fatigued		Mellow	Thoughtful	Peaceful	Comfortable	Carefree
Despairing	Hopeless	Desolate	Spent	Drained		Sleepy	Complacent	Tranquil	Cozy	Serene

Expected Outcomes: The Mood Meter is intended to assist your kids in developing ways for controlling (or regulating) moods. It gives them a "language" with which to express their emotions.

FUN ACTIVITY- Mirror Time

Dany: Let's have some fun with the mirror activity. Looking in the mirror is often associated with narcissism or self-doubt, but learning to view oneself in the mirror can promote self-compassion, managing stress, friendships, and emotional strength. It is in our nature to want to be seen and reflected. We learn to comprehend ourselves as kids by observing the reflections of people around us. Face-to-face interaction is critical for our psychological and social functioning. We miss out on social reflection as we spend so much time alone and on electronic devices. We can meet up with ourselves at any time by looking in the mirror.

What to do: Follow the to-do list in the worksheet below. Observe for 2 to five minutes. Write down what you noticed during observation. Then write about the thoughts that you had while looking in the mirror.

To Do's	What did you notice?	What were your thoughts?
Look at your face		
Look at your eyes		
Feel your Inner Critic		
Listen to your Thoughts		
Feel your emotions		
Look at your overall appearance.		

Talk to yourself about your face looks.		
Laugh and listen to your thoughts		
Observe your breath		
Notice your attention		

Expected Outcomes: Mirrors can trigger intense emotions in kids, but they can also be extremely effective instruments for shifting the kid's viewpoint and revealing aspects that are often hidden when they stare out into the world. Your kids will not become towering narcissists by learning to listen to their appearance. They will learn to stay present with themselves, moderate the strength of their feelings, and tap into a new inner power.

FUN ACTIVITY- Freeze Dance

Tip for Grown-Ups: Ask children to pause, take deep breaths, and, if possible, talk about their feelings when they start to feel strong emotions in other situations. If they cannot express their emotions verbally, have them "dance" them out. This freeze dance activity is a good idea for kids to let go of their emotional disturbance.

Jane: When my psychologist asked me to practice this activity, I played it with my mother. She helped me play and pause the different songs, and after my first try, I always got excited to try this activity with mom. Ask your parents to help you out with your freeze dance.

What to do: Find sad, happy, fast, slow, upbeat music etc. Move your body around and dance freely. Ask someone to stop the music after some time and change the beat. When the music stops, you need to record your emotions and thoughts. For each type of song, record everything. Dance on the upbeat first day, then move to sad other day and so on.

Song Type	Your Thoughts and Emotions

Expected Outcomes: This activity helps children develop and understand by expressing, analyzing, and controlling their emotions by moving and balancing their bodies with large muscles.

Self-Regulation through Fun Activities (Group)

FUN ACTIVITY- Duck-Duck Goose

Mia: Hey friend, Listen! Emotions are, by their nature, abstract. Identifying emotions can be difficult to teach, especially to young kids. For example, a student may be worried about an upcoming test or have fought with a sibling on the way to school. Learning about your emotions and how to regulate them is a vital first step.

What to do: Assume that you are a caller. We (Jane, Mia, and Dany) are other participants. We will sit in a circle (shown in the picture). Whenever you pass through us, you will tap our heads. And with tapping, you will call either duck or goose. If you call the duck by tapping on Jane's head, nothing will change, and you will move to Mia. But if you call the goose by tapping on Jane's head, Jane will chase you by running around the circle. You have to take over Jane's seat. If you sit on the seat, Jane will be the next caller. If Jane catches you and you cannot get the seat, you will sit in the center of the circle and be called Pot.

Expected Outcomes: Incorporating games into your kid's everyday routines can be a great self-regulating strategy. They will learn to calm down with these fun games. They will also enjoy other kids' company when they play relaxation and fun games with them.

FUN ACTIVITY- Partner Painting

Dany: Children's cooperative art activities are ideal for getting them to collaborate while also developing their visual-motor and motor skills. This enjoyable cooperative art activity encourages friends to collaborate and create matching paintings by following one another's example. I enjoyed doing partner painting with Jane and Mia when I was like you. We always had great fun doing all the stuff, and no doubt Mia was always painted beautifully. So, with whom are you going to paint?

What to do: I have given you a canvas for painting. Draw something you want to with your partner. Try to make one part by yourself and ask your partner to draw the other part on this canvas. Match them in the end and make a big painting.

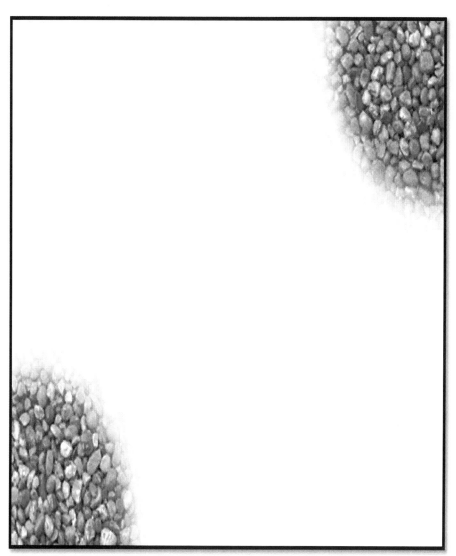

Expected Outcomes: The partner painting is a fun activity that allows kids to let go of their worries for some time and only focus on painting beautifully. Kids indulge in their arts and are most likely to let go of their negative world.

Self-Regulation through CBT Exercises

CBT EXERCISE- <u>Talking Back to Worries</u>

Jane: Worry may be a part of a child's daily life if they have learning difficulties. Is my work up to the mark? Is it possible that my classmates will think badly of me? Will I be able to pass this test? Will I be the last person chosen for the volleyball team? Understanding where worry emerges can help you manage these unpleasant, soul-crushing anxieties. The following are some suggestions for you to "talk back to worry" so that you can grow into a strong and healthy active learner.

What to do: Here, I have listed to-dos. Think of a situation. Then follow each step from above to below. For example, my situation is "My father does not give me enough time, but Sam's father always plays with him". In this situation, I have to understand what I am feeling sad about. The thing must be "my father's attention". To eliminate the worry, I will turn the negativity into positivity. Like, I hope my father will play with me after his work. To manage the worry, I will refine my statement. Like, my father's job must be a tough one. To focus on the thought, I will compare Sam's father's job with my father's job. And the process will keep going until you are satisfied with the situation. Try doing it in the worksheet below.

To Do's	Think of a situation happening in your life and proceed with the steps
Understand the situation	
Eliminate the worry	
Manage the worry	
Focus on your thoughts	

Choose to listen or ignore	
Set up your mind	
Plan your Actions	
Slow down and simplify things	
Take care of worry step-by-step	
Move forward little-by-little	
Track your progress	
Reach the final goal	

Expected Outcomes: The brain area most engaged at any given moment has a significant impact on behavior. Knowing how the mind operates and using tactics to help themselves gain power are important parts of helping a kid manage worry and anxiety. This activity works on the same rule. They will turn their worry into positive thoughts by themselves and will stick to it.

CBT EXERCISE- <u>The Feelings Remote Control</u>

Mia: When we are dealing with a very strong feeling, focusing on it can worsen. When we become worried, we are prone to obsessing, which is when we repeat fears repeatedly, intensifying them. Coping skills function as a remote control, allowing us to "change channels" on emotions by changing them to a different emotional state. The remote control also helps to "de-emphasize" an intense feeling to be more bearable. Most children are familiar with remote controls and how they operate.

What to do: I have a remote for you. You need to write down one strategy on each of your remote buttons. For example, Exercise, music, and guided visualization can help change the channel, so I will write it on the channel changing buttons. While relaxing methods such as inhaling and muscle relaxation can help tone down the volume, I will write it on lowering and raising volume buttons.

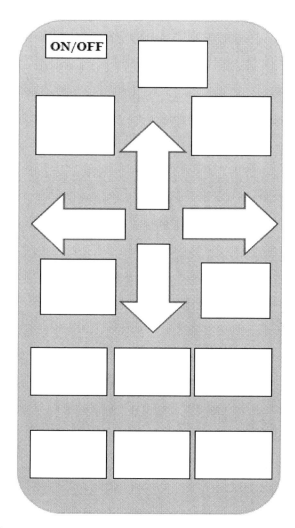

Expected Outcomes: The remote controls will make your kids follow a certain pattern for relaxation. Ask your kid to press down a button whenever he feels sad or depressed. Ask him to press the relaxation button when a relaxation exercise is needed.

CBT EXERCISE- <u>Looking Back, Looking Forward</u>

Dany: Looking back and looking forward is a very good idea to observe where you are now. Comparing ourselves with our past version always becomes a motivation for us.

<u>What to do</u>: Answer each statement by thinking carefully about yourself, what you wanted in the past and what you want now. In the end, tell me about your three most important future goals.

Looking Back	Looking Forward
What was I before?	What am I now?
My goal in life was	My goal in life now
I didn't like	Now I like
I played games	Now I play games
I mostly felt like	Now I feel
I wanted to become	Now I want to be
What I wanted to have	Now, I want to have
I struggled for	Now I am struggling for
I had friends (numbers)	Now I have friends

I loved to do	Now I love to do
My First Future Goal is	
My Second Future Goal is	
My Third Future Goal is	

Expected Outcomes: Looking Back, Looking Forward exercise will help you analyze your kid's current situation. How he was, how he is now and what he is thinking about his life. What goals he had made for himself and how much he is struggling. These all will help you understand your kid better and motivate them in his life goals.

CBT EXERCISE- If I were a Superhero

Jane: Here comes my favorite activity. We all have an image in mind for our superheroes, and we all want to become one. Now, tell me about your superhero viewpoints.

What to do: Fill out the questions asked in the picture below. Color the superhero and write your name on it.

Expected Outcomes: Learning lots of things can be hectic for kids. This activity is just for fun to calm down kids and think of themselves as a superhero. With this exercise, kids will recognize their worth and that they are not ordinary individuals. They are unique and have good intentions to help people with their superpowers. Tell your kids that helping others doesn't require superpowers. It requires only a strong heart and mind.

CBT EXERCISE- <u>Facing Fears</u>

Mia: If I tell you my experience, this exercise was very helpful for me. Back then, I had a lot of fears. For example, I always thought that my clothes did not suit me, and everyone stared at me when I walked into the classroom. I ranked it 9 out of 10. And then, my psychologist helped me make a plan to overcome this. So, I made a positive thought that everyone stared at me because I did not talk much with others and stayed quiet all time. Then I created a plan to talk to all my classmates gradually and became their friend. Do you want to know what happened next? Yes, I entered my class by looking and smiling at each of my classmates, and they also smiled in return every time. I overcame my fear with a simple plan, and I have so many examples. But I want you to try this for your fears.

What to do: Think of your fears and rank them out of 10 according to their intensity. Then make a plan to overcome that fear. Stick to it and wait for the results.

My Fears	Rank out of 10	My Plan to Overcome

Expected Outcomes: Overcoming fears is an important part of living a normal and healthy life. Kids will learn that every fear can be overcome, and it is not a big deal to work for their fears. With hard work and a smart plan, everything is achievable.

Self-Regulation through Relaxation Exercises

RELAXATION EXERCISE- <u>Wave Relaxation</u>

Dany: Now it is time for some relaxation exercises. What about water that gives us such a peaceful feeling? Water has been associated with rehabilitation and recovery since ancient times. Watching it wave and flow, listening to the sounds of the sea or a flowing river, or immersing our bodies in water may all help us relax and unwind. Ocean Breathing is one of yoga's most popular breathing techniques, combining deep breathing with the sound of the sea to promote peace, attention, clarity, and overall well-being. Ocean Breathing can be used to energize when practicing yoga positions and quiet and focus attention before relaxing.

What to do: Lie down on your back with your feet long and your arms at your sides, palms up. Help your body to fall to the floor by closing your eyes. Be completely still and silent. Connect to your breath by inhaling and exhaling slowly and deliberately. Allow your entire body to rest. Feel your abdomen and ribs expand as you inhale deeply and envision a wave pouring in and filling you up. Imagine yourself washed to shore by the waves and lying securely on a beach of nice, smooth, white sand. Allow yourself to sink completely into the sand underneath you. Take note of your feeling and write them down in the given section.

Let us know how you felt during the wave relaxing technique.

_____

_____

_____

_____

_____

_____

_____

Expected Outcomes: This exercise helps relax, de-stress, and calm your kids. As soon as they start doing this exercise, they will sink in their imagination while forgetting the stressful stuff.

RELAXATION EXERCISE- Floating Raft Relaxation

***Jane*:** Because these exercises are physical and accessible, travel visualizations are ideal for kids. You can float along a river, ride in a helium balloon over the sky, or experience floating on a cloud or in the air. Keep it basic and quick, around 3-5 minutes. With practice, you will be able to relax more. Try it in your room, before rest or sleep, or whenever you want to spend some quality time without getting anxious or worried.

What to do: Lie down on your back with your feet long and your arms at your sides, hands up. Help your body to fall to the floor by closing your eyes. Be completely still and silent. Answer the questions below when you are in a relaxed mood.
Is it possible for you to be so silent that you can sense your breathing?

_____

_____

Is it possible to be so still that you can feel your beating heart?

_____

_____

Are you floating down the beach or on a pond?

_____

_____

Now, think that a gentle breeze touches your face. You can feel the warmth of the sun on your skin. Feel the water moving beneath your raft in a gently rolling motion. On the raft, your entire body relaxes.

What do you think you smell?

As you float, what do you notice?

What noises do you hear in your near area?

Relax for as long as you want, then slowly wiggle your fingers and toes. Curl yourself into a small ball by hugging your knees to your chest. Give yourself a deep hug, then carefully roll to one side and sit up.

Expected Outcomes: The more your kids practice, the simpler it will become for them to relax. Kids will settle down more quickly and stay for longer periods.

RELAXATION EXERCISE- Affirmation Relaxation

Mia: Positive affirmations are an excellent way to retrain your subconscious mind to think positively instead of negatively. The aim is to repeat positive words about what you want to see to be developed in you until they become ingrained in your way of thinking.

What to do: To help you minimize stress, modify your thinking, and stay motivated, utilize the principles below to construct your own set of positive self-talk.

- **Your Intentions**

Consider what you are attempting to accomplish in your life. This involves focusing on the final result and the behaviors, attitudes, and characteristics you would like to acquire to get there. Answer the following questions.

Do you want to feel more at ease?

_____

_____

Do you want to develop healthy lifestyle habits?

_____

_____

Would you prefer to be a more supportive friend?

_____

_____

To figure out what's essential to you and get to the core of what you want to build in your life, you need to write it to brainstorm your mind. Write here.

_____

_____

_____

• Create Statements

Once you have a general notion of what you want to do, try to express it in a few basic sentences that reflect what you want to accomplish. Make the claims as if they are already true rather than if you want them to be true. "I am feeling calmer each day," for instance, would be preferable to "I wish to feel calmer." This is because you are teaching your subconscious mind to think the statements, which helps in their development. You are not attempting to desire something; rather, you are attempting to achieve it. Make your statement here.

_____

_____

_____

• Be Sure, they are Positive

If you are going to make positive affirmations, make sure they are positive. This implies expressing what you want to see and do rather than what you do not want to see and do. Instead of stating, "I don't want to feel stressed," or even "I'm no longer stressed," say, "I'm feeling calm." Your mind does not always detect the negative and instead hears the word "stress," which is exactly what you want to avoid.

Rewrite your statement in a positive way here.

_____

_____

_____

Expected Outcomes: Although not all positive affirmations are beneficial for adults (our minds may resist them if they are too unreal), they can assist your kids in getting into a better frame of mind and increase resilience and satisfaction in their lives. That's a lot of value for a small commitment of time. And, most of all, they are interesting.

RELAXATION EXERCISE- Belly Breathing Relaxation

Dany: It is simple to do belly breathing, and it is quite calming. If you need to relax or release tension, try this simple exercise.

What to do: In a relaxed place, sit or lie flat. Place one hand on your stomach, below the ribcage, and the other on your heart. Take a breath deeply and push your arm out with your belly. You must not lift your chest. As if you were blowing, exhale through pursed lips. Feel the palm on your tummy to go in and pull all the air out with it. Breathe in and out 5 to 10 times. Each breath should be taken slowly.

Take note of how you feel after doing the exercise.

_____

_____

_____

_____

_____

Expected Outcomes: All of these exercises will help your kids unwind and rest. Breathing exercises can assist them in relaxing since they simulate how the body feels. The way you breathe has an impact on your entire body. Breathing exercises can help your kids relax, calm, and relieve stress. Breathing exercises are simple to pick up. They can be performed wherever your kids need, and they don't require any particular tools.

RELAXATION EXERCISE- Dragon Breaths

Jane: Dragons are one of the most well-known mythological creatures on earth, and they have captivated the minds of people worldwide. People thought dragons were real in medieval times and that dinosaur bones were evidence of their existence. But this dragon breaths exercise is not about dragons. It is a relaxation technique that can take up your mind, boost your energy, improve your attention and concentration, soothe anxiety, reduce stress, and positively impact every organ in your body.

What to do: Sit cross-legged or take a knee with your back straight. Inhale deeply through your nose. Exhale slowly and noisily through your mouth. You have the option of sticking your tongue out and widening your eyes and mouth. As you breathe, raise or lower your hands like dragon wings. Repeat 3-5 times faster.

Take note of how you feel after doing the exercise.

_____

_____

_____

_____

Expected Outcomes: Tension and negative thinking are released with Dragon Breathing. It is a wonderful activity to do when your kids are furious or feel like they are about to lose control. A few rounds of dragon breath can be enough to help them relax.

RELAXATION EXERCISE- Mindful Breathing

Mia: Taking a few minutes to practice mindful breathing can make a significant impact on your day. The practice of mindful breathing might help you build a habit and grow more comfortable with it. What matters is that you practice it. It is a tool that you can use to pull yourself back to the present in difficult events, and who wouldn't want such a useful tool on hand? It is simple to learn mindful breathing, and it is as simple as taking another breath.

What to do: It might sometimes be good to start with an extended breath: a deep intake through your nose (2 seconds), keep your breath (3 seconds), and a prolonged exhale through your mouth, particularly when trying to calm oneself in a stressful situation (5 seconds). You may notice that your attention wanders due to thoughts or body sensations as you do so. It will be ok. You would become aware of this and gradually bring your attention back to your breathing.
Take note of how you feel after doing the exercise.

_____

_____

_____

_____

Expected Outcomes: Setting out a certain time for this exercise might be beneficial, but it can also be beneficial to perform it when your kids are feeling especially stressed or nervous. Experts believe that practicing mindful breathing regularly will simplify doing so under stressful situations.

RELAXATION EXERCISE- Progressive Muscle Relaxation

Dany: I am giving you the last relaxation exercise. Progressive muscle relaxation (PMR) is a profound way to relax that has been shown to alleviate the symptoms of severe pain and regulate tension and anxiety. Progressive muscle relaxation is founded on the premise concept of clenching (or tightening) one muscle group at a time, then relaxing and releasing the tension.

What to do: Contract one muscular group (for instance, your lower thighs) for ten seconds while breathing, then breathe and relieve the tension in that muscle group quickly. Allow up to 10 seconds for relaxation before moving onto another muscle group. Take note of the changes you experience as the muscle group releases while eliminating the tension. Assuming that tense feelings are flowing out of your mind as you stretch each muscle group may be beneficial in connection with the relief of stress. Gradually tense and relax muscle groups as you make your way up the body.

Take note of how you feel after doing the exercise.

_____

_____

_____

_____

_____

Expected Outcomes: For relieving symptoms in various illnesses, such as migraines, neuropathic pain, hypertension, and digestive disorders, physicians have utilized relaxation exercises in combination with traditional therapy. This will help your kids during the same symptoms to be calm and relaxed.

FEEDBACK

Hey Kid! At the end of your self-regulation journey, Jane, Mia, and Dany have some questions from you.

Which activity did you like the most? Why?

_____

_____

_____

_____

Which activity helped you out most of all?

_____

_____

_____

_____

Which activity did you enjoy the most?

_____

_____

_____

_____

Which activity was boring? Why?

_____

_____

_____

_____

_____

Which activity made you laugh the most?

_____

_____

_____

Which exercise was very difficult?

_____

_____

_____

Who helped you out in most of your activities and exercises?

_____

_____

_____

Do you want to say something to us (Jane, Mia, and Dany)?

_____

_____

_____

The Takeaway Message

You may think that there are times when it is preferable to keep your child away from distressing situations. If you notice a sad video is being shown, for instance, you can persuade your child to skip it if you know they will have trouble pulling themselves together afterward.

Maybe you are thinking of letting your child miss a school trip day because you know they have a hard time controlling their emotions, and you are afraid they will lose control if their volleyball team loses the game. While it may sound appealing, a circumstance like this is certain to arise at some point in one's life, and practicing managing it, can be extremely beneficial.

Remember that there is a huge beneficial side to emotional regulation, and change can happen anytime. Children who have strong emotions are likely to experience a wide range of emotions. This means that, in the morning, your excessively emotional youngster may be enraged, but in the evening, they may also be compassionate or a strong leader. When kids are experiencing irritation, they may also experience pleasure and excitement after some time.

Excluding your child from every difficult obstacle or all of life's truths is ineffective. Your kid needs some practice handling a range of emotions in various circumstances for their development and standard of living. Instead of protecting kids from all painful situations, make sure you give them plenty of chances to handle their big feelings.

Remember that managing one's emotions involves awareness and skill set those young kids still acquire. Even so, being highly emotional is a natural trait for some children. All they may need is a little additional assistance, guidance, and tolerance from you to learn how to manage their emotions appropriately. The process can be difficult at times, but the effort you put in will benefit your child for the rest of their life. Consider emotions to be the flavor of life and our capacity to control them to be comparable to being a chef. Great chefs don't hide away from specific flavors; instead, they appreciate, comprehend, and find a way to work with them. Flavors, like feelings, can be mild or powerful. You do not want the flavor to overrun your meal, so you keep it under control, resulting in a much better overall experience.

There are various advantages to having better emotion management tactics to take care of your emotions. Individuals who practice emotional management are healthier and better manage life's difficulties. Emotion regulation is a protective measure against anxiety and depression. Furthermore, kids who can manage their emotions have greater flexibility in thinking and higher focus, emotion regulation, and problem-solving abilities. These advantages have a ripple effect, resulting in more self-assurance, emotional well-being, and general satisfaction.

Made in United States
Troutdale, OR
07/06/2023

11022355R00075